GIVE OVER, GRAYMALKIN

Give Over, Graymalkin

Gaylord Brewer

POEMS

RED HEN PRESS | *Pasadena, CA*

Book design and layout by Kathrine Davidson

Library of Congress info:

Brewer, Gaylord, 1965-

  Give Over, Graymalkin: poems / Gaylord Brewer.—1st ed.

  p. cm.

  ISBN 978-1-59709-493-1

  I. Title.

  PS3552.R4174G58 2011

  811'.54—dc22

  2010049017

The Los Angeles County Arts Commission, the National Endowment for the Arts, the California Arts Council, and Department of Cultural Affairs City of Los Angeles partially support Red Hen Press.

First Edition

Published by Red Hen Press

www.redhen.org

ACKNOWLEDGMENTS

Many of these poems were written during three residencies: at La Muse in southern France and later that summer in Cherbourg; as a fellow at the Global Arts Village in Delhi, India; and during a second stay, thirteen years after the first, at the Fundación Valparaíso in southeast Spain. Whatever the result, I thank the kind folks who took care of me during these travels. Thanks also to Middle Tennessee State University for a Non-Instructional Assignment, a Faculty Development Grant, and a Faculty Research and Creative Activities Committee Grant that allowed for the completion of this manuscript. For her assistance with and information regarding the frontispiece (a woodcut from a 1544 edition on witchcraft), I'm indebted to Marina Zurkow.

Finally, kudos to the editors of the following journals where most of these poems appeared in various forms. *Alimentum*: "Fête de l'Indépendance (or, July 4th, Final Evening in France)," "Sunday, Another Week of Life Spent"; *Argestes*: "Dead Metaphor: Day Lilies," "Dead Metaphor: Illness"; *Briar Cliff Review*: "Dead Metaphor: Infidelity"; *The Cape Rock*: "The Months," "Swami Keerti Reminds Me that I Am God and Suggests a Bedtime Meditation"; *Common Ground Review*: "Dead Metaphor: Home"; *Connecticut Review*: "New Year's Eve, India"; *Carolina Quarterly*: "Hymn of the Flies"; *Chautauqua Literary Journal*: "A History of Flamingos"; *The Dark Horse* (Scotland): "The Whiskies of Nainital"; *Evansville Review*: "Everywhere"; *Freshwater*: "Three Nights, and One Other," "To the Wind"; *Greensboro Review*: "Another Good Friday, Good Death"; *Grist*: "Hunting the Python with Mr. Singh," "Jungle Appetites"; *Indiana Review*: "Dead Metaphor: Fidelity," "Dead Metaphor: The Number Thirteen," "The Whiskies of Nainital"; *Iron Horse Literary Review*: "Dead Metaphor: Learning the Bicycle"; *Jelly Bucket*: "Upon the Third Day Returned to France, at the Old Church on the Hill," "What the Rain Taught"; *The Listening Eye*: "Dead Metaphor: Bullfighting" (Sports Poem Contest Winner), "Dead Metaphor: Day Lilies"; *Louisville Review*: "Barbaro," "Dead Metaphor: The Champagne Toast," "Dead Metaphor: The Rose"; *Mid-American Review*: "Heart's Warning"; *Muse & Stone*: "Dead Metaphor: Clouds"; *Natural Bridge*: "Dead Metaphor: Pregnant Wife," "To the Wind"; *New Delta Review*: "Dead Metaphor: Mosquitoes as Nazis"; *New Madrid:* "Dead Metaphor: Sunlight after Morning Thunder"; *North American Review*: "A Small, Gone Moment"; *Notre Dame Review*: "Lost Poem Regarding the Musée d'Orsay, Rescued by Renoir," "Probably Human"; *Oyez Review*: "Lovemaking,"

"Small Mercy"; *RE: Arts & Letters*: "Do Not," "Midnight, December 31, 2006"; *Reed Magazine*: "Dead Metaphor: Post-Divorce Harley-Davidson"; *River Styx*: "After Buying a Rabbit at the Carcassonne Market," "Beginning New Year's Day with Swami Keerti's Laughing Meditation"; *St. Petersburg Review*: "Scalloping," "Swami Keerti Surprises Me by Using the Word 'Bullshit' on Christmas"; *Santa Clara Review*: "Calling My Mother from India"; *The Southern Review:* "After"*; Studio One*: "Dead Metaphor: Clouds"; and *Yemassee:* "Jasper."

For—
Lucy: damn, kid, just in time.
And the comely "wife character."

In memory—
Robert Culp and Robert B. Parker,
two of the last ones.
And Rane Arroyo.

TABLE OF CONTENTS

IV: The Dead Metaphors

V: Otra Vez

AFTER

What did they portend,
the commotion and hunger,
the overnight trains

twisted in hot sheets?
What the late arrivals
and the taxis, always a taxi,

bartered and argued?
Dim light—for the best—
in those dim rooms.

They caged the cold
in winter, heat in summer.
What was the tally,

bills exchanged,
counted to waiting palms,
money lost and another

dirty stack, extracted
somehow? Enough to get by,
get along. So you got by,

got along, is that it?
How did they accrue,
handshakes, confidences,

faces distorted above flame?
All soon forgotten.
Rare moments better,

standing privately
under the nights, a glass,
glitch of calm, answering

again failures and omissions.
The moon's penumbras,
the village fires,

the river ruminations—
these were what you paid for,
they knew to listen

and too were forgotten.
What was a life worth,
beleaguered friend,

when you finally returned,
stinking, unshaven,
parched all the way through?

Dark doorway and key,
hand pushing forward,
one step across to silence.

I: In the Gaze of Swami Keerti

I'm a holy man minus the holiness.
    —E. M. Forster

COME WITH ME

Beneath the simmering moon,
one phase off full, perhaps—
for our work round and rich enough.
Ignore the flight to Bombay
or Sri Lanka. Let the new year

begin here. We'll resolve
if violet sky is velvet or bruise.
Stand with me where lunging bats,
wide as our two spread hands,
break the lake into dark circles.

The black peripheral trill,
near collision and spinning rapture—
too much spin, you say, to believe?
Listen: Long before we met
I longed to bring you to this place.

Hear bamboo acrobatic above
our heads? Don't be afraid.
Bats specialize in frantic hunger.
Tonight, I promise your new name—
Monisha, Deeha, Shanti?—

when again the moment arrives
to speak. Come. Trust me.
Not even a whisper now. Be still.
Just our shared breathing,
ignited in the feasting night.

JUNGLE APPETITES

—Corbett Tiger Reserve, Uttaranchal

At last I had shed the cooks and porters,
slipped guide and driver to get where I shouldn't.
Leaving the road for that enticing artery of dirt,
chance greeting desire. Human world
soon mute, I followed this sharper attentiveness,
canopy of neem and pine. Elephant dung marked
the way. I kicked apart one clay-like brick.
Strawy warmth, halo of gnat, inarguable
musky perfume. Black-faced langurs swung ahead.
When I rousted the sambar buck, elk-like,
chestnut-dark, and watched its wide crown
disappear, I equally startled. Otherwise,
the quiet was exquisite, late afternoon light
angled and rich—my three shirts too many layers
for temperate winter. What I am saying,
even in the dry riverbed, studying a mishmash
of deer and boar hooves, elephant tracks deep
and large as serving plates, even as I prayed not to
find what I sought and found, I felt no fear.
My late, heavy lunch, first meat I'd taken
in weeks, jostled in my stomach. I wasn't armed,
of course, except with weariness. Nothing
threadbare as bravery involved itself. I'm saying
that as I crouched before the wide indention
of pugmark, recent fossil fine in sand, unmarred
between rock, I felt only calm exhilaration,
a stupid, fateful surety. Life was grand, absurd.
The tiger could have me if it wanted. I wouldn't
embarrass us with resistance. I had delivered myself,
my own meal undigested. I apologized to wife,

mother, but I'd witnessed worse fates lately.
From the spidering crux of an immense banyan,
I watched the light move and tried to listen.
And not until I had chosen to continue,
entered a head-tall blind of grass, blades enveloping,
touching, hushing me, did I feel a frisson
of panic, sweet trembling bloom, hear the drum
and bellows of heart and lungs. All the easy,
mournful luck of my life, announcing to the wild.

Do Not

Do not come for me
with tributes of bread
and tea. Do not, I ask politely,

bring fist against
my bolted door,
call my name to raise me.

Do not unfold
your explanations of the night,
petition my alliance

or my company.
Do not, for my own good,
rouse me to clocks

and mirrors.
Please, too, refrain
from custodial

attentions—rechecking
of outlets and bulbs,
short broom

to sweep my floor clean
of what has fallen,
pages of discarded news

to polish windows.
You are kind, let us assume,
but I see well enough

the ceaseless day beyond
curtained frame,
unveiled when I choose.

Here cool water
in a pitcher,
drawn before the crush

of voices resumed.
If you care for me, offer only
your absence.

CALLING MY MOTHER FROM INDIA

I punch in the Hindi figures
and, amazingly, a muted ring begins.
Eight thousand miles away
in Kentucky, my mother lifts

the receiver in a mottled hand
and asks hello. She is surprised, happy—
it is her baby, after all—but I hear
too her slight disorientation,

taint of worry about my choices.
I play the part, explain I am sitting
beneath a square of mosquito netting,
speak of goat-brain curry,

great bats that circled my head
and, with a slightly cheating flourish,
of nine-foot spitting cobras
discovered in Kenya, each

with venom enough to kill fifteen men.
My god, she says, *isn't that where
you are?* I regret the cobras
and make assurances. Back on topic:

the house is finally decorated,
the family is coming
for Christmas on the 22nd.
Goldie's husband recovers poorly

from his stroke and this call
is costing me a fortune. The echoes,
stalls, hollows make joking difficult.
I hear my voice, stiff and loud.

My brother's just walked in
for a visit and says hi. My father
wants fucking sweetener for his cereal.
Seconds and rupees gone forever,

dispensed to black infinity,
babel until pink packets are found.
I'm don't mention the sadness
that has just come over me,

a palpable wave, frail cloth,
thickness I can taste. Instead, I stress
to this aging woman I love
that all is well, then get fancy

and note that it is late here,
that I've lived already through
their Sunday morning. Too much.
I miss her. I'm tired and should go.

Once more she mentions the cost
as if some haunting abstraction,
a loss beyond human recovery—
no one expects to hear from me again.

SWAMI KEERTI REMINDS ME THAT I AM GOD AND SUGGESTS A BEDTIME MEDITATION

God is going to sleep now.
He tilts water from a pitcher,
lowers mesh around His bedding
and is more than happy to put
a stupid, wasted day behind Him.
He remains concerned, however,
by a stubborn chill and slight fever,
by the gaseous result of the soda
He drank for His stomach. Troubled,
also, by the raw anger He feels
for a bad choice manipulated into.
He strives against dualities, but He's tired.
God listens to His breathing
and nods into a sweaty trance of sleep.

At the mirror, dreamy for fried eggs
and worried if my Delhi liquor stall
will be open on Christmas, staring into
bloodshot eyes, I realize I have
utterly forgotten to awaken slowly,
listen passively to sounds of morning
I cannot control, feel God arriving
within me. Shit. I think for a moment,
seduced by the mind, and decide
it's too late to go back to bed. The boy
trots by ringing the breakfast bell—
no time even to sit beneath the banyan
and salvage some feeble aura.
No choice now but toast, tepid Nescafé,
an early rickshaw to fetch whisky
for the coming party. Luckily for me,

Swami is a generous, fine-humored man,
appreciative certainly of both attempt
and wretched failure. Don't be greedy
about godliness, he reminded me,
also that the first taste will be tiny.
But, apparently, sweet and addictive.
God reminds Himself tonight's another night
and tomorrow, Christmas, another day
of spirited, joyful consciousness. Why not?

Swami Keerti Surprises Me by Using the Word "Bullshit" on Christmas

Meditation is the only
alchemy, and "all else
in the name of alchemy
is just bullshit, occult nonsense,
esoteric rubbish."
He goes on to elucidate
a consciousness beyond
birth and death, but I'm stopped
by the word, pondering
translations, tonal slippage,
reminded too of the jarring
Indian use of "slut."

As in, say: "The Mughul Emperor,
scoffing at the thought
of the prince his son's
advancing troops
finely bedecked atop
golden-tusked elephants,
spent the night before
the slaughter—that morning
when the Jumna ran red
with his ended reign—
in the imperial fort,
drinking wine and carousing
with his harem of sluts . . ."

Anyway, before I can
resolve the linguistics
and stifle a cringe,
Swami's glowing

green orbs lock on me.
It's time to cease thinking
and purely, simply "be."
Even his white beard radiates joy
this Christmas morning,
and, no bullshit, robed arms
spread again into the wings
of an eternal hug.

The Whiskies of Nainital

Sixty-three kilometers of rising switchback
from Ramnagar, then steeply by foot or horse
to Naini Peak until the Himalayan ridge
snags you on its jagged, ethereal smile—
who may blame the traveler for his thirst?
Those flush may consider, at a princely 125 rupees,
a peg of *Teachers 50* or, blunt and beguiling,
Something Special, while the humbler seeker may
follow mystery or imagination—*Soulmate Premium*,
Utopia, the monstrous promises of *Sangrila*.
Highland moors bellow with *Royal Stag*,
brave *Petter Scot*, a tonic of *Bagpiper Prestige*.
Imperial blood flames again with paradox
in a dram or three of *New Imp. Old Res.* (a crime
of a bargain at 15 rupees), steeds glisten in
luminous tumblers of *Derby Special,* the fox flees
a dyslexic rush of *Aristrocate* (20 rupees).
The festivities of *Beach House*, meanwhile,
an ambiguous season of *Summer Holl*, we leave
to the impetuous and the foolhardy.

Perusing the folio of titles, please remember
mostly the parched *spirit* will be fulfilled.
That the Gods' share of these ambrosias exists
only on paper, greet as caveat and blessing.
Myths of clear distillation—a simple trinity
of vodka (*Magic Woman, Romonov*, the lubricating
Fuel Fuel) or one crystal gin, *Blue Ribond Tango*
(25 rupees), inspire in kind. As for rum
and for the body, perhaps a flask of *Old Monk*
may exist for the coins from a dusty purse,

although of *8 P.M. Bermuda*, the winsome
Honey Bee, only tales remain. So accept
what is offered from its monastic shelf,
sit back in the fading day, peer at an icy cube
as to a diminished future. Below, the priests
of Sri Ma Naini Temple raise the evening chant.
Gondoliers cross the lake in somber return.
And you, lifting to cracked lips this cool amber,
a double peg "long aged, very excellent"
of *Old Smuggers*—that's what the label says.

New Year's Eve, India

At last, cease-fire with the workers,
agreement for quiet mornings.
I feel responsible to speak something
into this gift of bartered silence,
fix some small permanence

in the moment or just make a racket.
If this were my call to you, yes,
I could confirm that I remain in India.
A kitten saunters past the screen,
then the other looking for trouble,

neither seeing me. Voice, birdcall,
pliant shadow of leaves on my hand.
Nothing you haven't heard.
I might remind you Aries' dance
is the vigorous Merengue, yours, Libra,

the happy and expressive Rumba,
or confirm our two years of pain.
Improbably, even announce
a stubborn light bastarding through
clouds we thought might never lift.

I'm comfortable here, oddly peaceful.
The body feels good, perseveres.
We've no champagne for midnight
so kindly drink a toast for me,
and if it pleases you raise a pledge.

I'll settle for the quiet. Arcing bats,
the genial arrival of the dark.
The musk of fires, beyond these walls
faint music that, despite myself,
I am beginning to hear again.

Beginning New Year's Day with Swami Keerti's Laughing Meditation

> So, when you wake up in the morning, the first thing
> to do is to start laughing consciously. Though you as
> well as others may not think very highly of your mental
> sanity, do not allow these perceived notions of madness
> to impede laughter.

The science feels soft—laughter healthier
than jogging—but who would argue against
"regulated hormones" or a "strengthened
immunity"? Swami's been good for me,
so I part curtains, lock doors and windows,
and start laughing my ass off. I am standing,
so to enable unimpeded breath-flow in the body,
and pad the room in crazy-eights, honking
like a sick duck of some soon-extinct species—
say, the blue-necked Tibetan booby.
All this distracting movement, I decide,
is generating too much extraneous thought,
so I drop to my floor pillow, cross my legs
between a few buttery fingers of sun.
Still, the effect falls short of utter joy, closer
to that diesel Volkswagen from graduate school,
hacking through every morning below 40° F.
Then the racket in my throat morphs
into a noise of lament—whining, stifled hiccups.
I try to conjure an absurd image and come up
with this: me sitting on a floor in India
forcing maniacal stutters, a few select and
hung-over friends watching and shaking heads.
Osho maintained laughter is the highest
spiritual quality, lacking from most religion,
so I sputter along, try to crank the motor
to ignition, raise the booby in a splashy ascent,

keeping just a little lid on the ruckus
so the girl who cleans my room won't hear.
She's newly eighteen and out there somewhere.
At last, the effort peters out into sudden
and I hope meditative silence. I close eyes
and enter my being, barge right in. I feel alright,
tight in the abs, light-headed, foolish in the sense
of pleased fool and seeker. I'm going home,
Swami Keerti, and however your lessons travel,
I thank you. And wish you much amusement.

HUNTING THE PYTHON WITH MR. SINGH

You sensed my disappointment, Mr. Singh,
    with the spoonbill, black-necked crane,
sleeping nightjar. *Very good view.* Maybe
    nineteen years of jungle service warned you

I needed more than migrating Siberian bee-eater,
    more even than eagle owl chick peering
with full-moon eyes from its high roost. *Got'm?*
    Neither jackal nor nilgai antelope sufficed.

What chance parakeet, humble ibis, even
    dazzling kingfisher—*got'm?* Yet you wouldn't be
dismissed, were mystified by my desire to ramble.
    Without me you don't see nothing. Understand?

Your insistence I use your binoculars
    and leave my small pair dangling, your contained
fascistic peddling of bicycle—*left side in India!*—
    as I wobbled behind. Every assertion

I was in charge making it clearer I wasn't.
    You hunted to secure your point, commission
for tiger, leopard, rhino. I had your card.
    We'll have python another day, I suggested,

hopeless on the pinching seat. *We have python today!*
    Maybe you did want that snake for me too.
But Mr. Singh, did we have to hike
    every pockmarked, lunar plane in the reserve,

study every desolate scrub and deserted burn,
      for four more hours raise the earth's choking dust?
Did we have to kneel at *every* black hole
      wide as a human leg? *Sun no good. Understand?*

Gleeful for any half-baked excuse, I understood.
      Even you, Mr. Singh, at last had no choice
but to accept termination of your service.
      Pay what I am worth, you announced

over my shoulder, toward the drained wetlands
      —*local politics!*—into blank sky once raucous
with 10,000 painted storks. I handed over the dingy
      bills, which you counted with a twitch of lip

before folding precisely into the pocket
      of your khakis. Maybe it was petty of me
not to buy you that beer. We wouldn't be
      seeing any leopards. Rhinos either. Understand?

II: Last Days

> . . . but what good will it do us,
> the closeness of a grave?
> —*Pablo Neruda*

EVERYWHERE

As if, for example, I were to step
into your mother's silent room
to sharpen nub of pencil, mind on clock
and the sentence of the day,
and find on her desk two photographs.

The first perhaps at the old house
we rented, you brushed, strong,
glowing in sunlight and shadow,
attentive to some good possibility beyond
the polished frame.

The second, say, amber and unfocused
in your mother's lap, her smile for you,
yours for me. The last Christmas,
days after the bad surgery, the blood,
together in our warm home.

You were leaving us already, pal.
If she were to sleeve this moment
in plastic, I would know the simple why
of that, that much at least—
so to kiss your face without harm.

THREE NIGHTS, AND ONE OTHER

Each morning, through blur
of eyes I stepped evenly from stone
to stone, careful regard
not to further disturb the world.
Those hours at work, the calls,
the furious drive home. Each afternoon
for three days she carried you to me.

On the first day the tanagers arrived,
their caustic back and forth
announcing geography out of whack.
He black-winged, crimson-flash
in high foliage, she olive-drab, smaller.
Each sundown, briefcase emptied,
shifted to a soft shirt,
I hunted them, focused elusive shapes
in a wet frame of lens.
I was mad for augury, for sign,
some meaning for hell.
Each night for three we arranged
your sweet, painful bones in my arms.
I took the licks and soft nibbles
delivered to nose and cheek,
the recant of every bite, all a kindness.

The morning after the fourth night
I was free, no office to attend.
We'd never heard tanagers here before,
haven't again since I buried you.

MIDNIGHT, DECEMBER 31, 2006

Who but fool or martyr raises fist
as if a moon recalled losses, cared
for anything than tattered finery of cloud
and not that either. Where I'd cloaked you
in one blanket of cotton, one of earth,
where what remains of your body rests
without pain, I bowed. No fancy words,
sweet boy, not for us, just promises,

hushed apologies, the wailing I've made
my art for the half of an unforgiven year.
And rifle shots close for company,
same hunters who rouse your mother
from our cold bed these Sunday mornings.
Tonight, their random fire delivers
one wounded year to the next, the first
of all remaining when I won't see you.

THE MONTHS

Part of me, jagged piece but admitted,
rejoiced to remove the year from its nail,
its weepy days, blank months.
December's Arctic fox just too much
of you to stand—plush broom of tail,
pointed ears, dark eyes in white.

Not you, of course, but constant visitor
to this chair where I face wall and window
beneath which you lie in winter.
So I folded away that wretched year,
the damned year that ruined us. But I ask truly,
what hope renews? January's polar bear

pensive and gentle with her cubs,
Feb.'s snow leopard and tufted, kitten-cute
brood? Puppy, is there anywhere,
from the drilled North to the melted Bering,
to the desecrated Himalayas, where
a beautiful ghost won't take my breath?

Another Good Friday, Good Death

It was easy: staring stonily into the ice-splintered sea
of the glass, the cold anchor of a speared olive,
ass adjusted to jagged cushion of rock amid a garden
of skull and shards. Always easy: to toast his own

mutilation, so natural, engraved epitaph of want.
So right, old hound stationary and cautious of falling,
snout west toward all that passes, panting smile
to greet a breeze that, while merely echo of storm,

still trembles just-greening crosses of limbs.
The man allows himself a smile, too, recollection
of the five dollars dispensed earlier in coin,
twenty clinking pieces to a precise, mechanical purse.

So seductive, to let it go, one's life for a meager price,
and to play both roles—for what friend might one trust
with betrayal? Resurrection was the bother:
the bitch, the bear, hammer, impossible chestnut.

Now, cool liquid holy on his lips, clear blood.
In three days she'd be home, these holidays passed over.
He'd rise rotting from their bed, loose the tatters
of a soiled shroud, scatter himself across her like ash.

THE BOUNTY OF EASTER

As I pass in a red flush of speed,
The Church of Christ reminds me
not only that He Is Risen
but that when it's dark I should
head for the Son.

All afternoon I've attempted just that,
driving hard, my cropped head exposed
to 89 unseasonal degrees and robes to a fist of wind.
The young man at Oil & Lube questioned the judgment
of the top down, but I explained to the child
that it was April, no choice, and paid in cash.

Soon church and flashing school zone
are behind. I accelerate, nowhere and nothing to hide,
race to preserve on the seat a sackful
of price-reduced chocolate eggs, in the slaughterhouse
trunk seven, yes seven legs of post-resurrection lamb
purchased for a carnivore's song.

Beyond that, much remains uncertain,
although I can almost guarantee,
as I sling a first cool haunch, five days from expiration,
onto my shoulder and slouch toward our sanctuary
of refrigerated shelves, soon bowed,
that somebody's sure to get his hands bloody,
somebody to raise a blade, and a toast,
as the lion lies down to eat.

LOVEMAKING

You startled me by how you took me,
your ferocity, your delicious taboo,
laughing lioness to my stunned and dripping
wildebeest. But I'm no boy scout, *simba*,
responded with a fiery comeback,
pouncing of my own, some claw and snout.

So naturally I was dismayed when I woke,
arms numb beneath my ridiculous walrus body,
unmovable. Two feet away you slept.
In the pale dawn, I studied your parted lips,
the trembling screens of your eyelids—
crept onto you, determined to thrust the vision
into the real, to breach those worlds.

But when I opened eyes again,
arms still immobile, the distance to your face
remained. Why these comatose
inducements, these drugged tumblings?
I strained to overwhelm, to ravage, at least
to close the space. Then I woke a third time,
a blur, too far to feel your breath,
and when I pronounced your name, and failed,
my voice was darkness.

By inhuman effort, I heaved the stone
of my body away from you,
toward whatever remained of the dream.

BARBARO

By second replay of his reigned, fraught stumble
across combed track, ankle flapping horribly wrong
angles, I realize I am sitting in the same chair,
my wife on the cushion of loveseat, as the morning
the towers collapsed. When I look, she is crying again.
I have set my glass on its coaster although
I do not remember this. I recognize a dense,
liquified quality to the air, the unfamiliar aspect
of my living room, prints and paintings hung straight,
photograph of stallions galloping in moonlight
Claudia's since childhood. We've no classes today,
as we did then, this being Saturday and summer,
time of ease and sport, but agree without speaking
to dress and find a crowd. The drive, too, mostly silent.
Before we leave, on-line reports already conjecture
"multiple fractures," "please pray," and worse.
When we stop at the Indians' store for forgotten wine,
I wait outside. At remodeled Bangkok Cuisine,
I can't drink, can't swallow the inky Tempranillo,
eat without incident lemongrass and coconut milk soup,
phad thai with fried tofu, my wife's favorite meal.
It does taste good. I ingest most of what's put before me
and manage one churlish monologue about infants
and parents being allowed in public, or even to live.
We admire the hardwood floors installed (bargain
at a rumored $30,000) by the chef's husband
and polished to such sheen the planks seem fabricated.
For no good reason, I tuck my fortune into a pocket
without sharing, although immediately I've forgotten
its instruction. Then we tip heavily and can go.
Here is what I'm telling you: We cork a nearly full bottle

and I steer carefully, car top up, though I do feel
one moment of illogical panic as to the dog's welfare.
Home. No news on the internet. We watch
the end of a laugher TV disaster movie, earthquake
cracking California to island, go to bed facing oppositely.
And the last of it: Long window dressings of lightning.
For hours, artillery of thunder rattling empty sky.
What, finally?: At 3:47 a.m. rain and hail arrived, siege
on the house began. I heard hooves against our roof,
gutters overwhelmed, and suppose Claudia did, too.
The Gods of War. Were there ever another kind?

SUNDAY, NIGHT

Yes, I nearly dubbed it Sabbath,
as I remain in a portentous
and self-indulging mood.
But when I woke in the dark
in confusion, midnight
one minute passed, no longer shivering,
I rose to free myself
from wool socks and cotton legs.
Safe again in blankets
I found you suddenly there,
with nothing in the winter world
like your dog close in bed,
and our faint god allowed me
a few scenes of untainted memory,
good romp and play.
In the late, gray room I heard
your mother turn, and turn again,
and knew her night wasn't
so merciful. But you stayed for awhile,
with nothing more to pay,
and when sleep returned
you were, naturally, right with me
loping behind that pale curtain.

III: South to North

Give over, Graymalkin, there are
horsemen on the road with horns
of fire, with withy roods.
    —*Cormac McCarthy*

Upon the Third Day Returned to France, at the Old Church on the Hill

You had examined already
the archway of locked doors,
cemetery tributes,
careful rows of slate tile
rough and cold.
Lowered one branch then another
of unknown flowering tree
to breathe its meaning,
passed chestnuts patterning
earth with busted
knots of thorn. Having not
found what you weren't
seeking you returned
to sentinels of cedar iridescent
with mold, fingered
damp trunks that gave
no secrets, returned down the path
toward the next village.
Why not the flattened corpse
of a red squirrel
caught dead in surprise?
Skewed teeth with no
bite, tufted ears hearing nothing.
Isn't that the way, the lesson
that announces and explains you?
By brush of tail
turn the body,
study an operation of ants
through socket and nostril.
Still by the tail, peeling

remains from unpaved road,
send it over the wall
to a final bed of fern,
feel suddenly at home.

To the Wind

You are the muscled silence
that roughs the world to sound.
Waves growling and aroused,
ripe applause of olive grove,
cool gossip between cedars,
whispering mountain rose, prickly
and languorous. I too am nearly
defenseless to your bullying
as you articulate the sail of my shirt
fiercely across chest and plane
a quiet, urgent lyric over cheek.

I'm nearly upended, but not quite,
unlike the shutter you rudely
slap open and shut all night long,
until exhausted on its hinge.

AFTER BUYING A RABBIT AT THE CARCASSONNE MARKET

> He wants to die
> like a rabbit, and he wants me
> to help him.
> —*Philip Levine*

Again I got what I'd claimed
to want—how to get rid of it?
Four days surviving
on hard bread, sticky jam,
coffee and cheap wine fueled
a *marché* thrill for *le lapin*.
Now I stood in sandals
and woolen socks
in a kitchen shared by strangers—
body parts, blood and goo
on my hands. Divide hind legs
from back, heart from liver,
seal for another day.
Okay. Until smaller upper
thighs, oddly distended,
showed halves of a severed face.
I paused, but so what?
With dull communal blade
I attacked each portion of neck,
sawed and twisted
until both half-heads, mushy-
fleshed and bone-sharp, separated.
I couldn't help spreading
tiny-toothed jaws with a thumb,
softly touching each soft,
opaque, sightless eye.
Well, I'd wasted a lot lately,
and I wanted a lot.

Even so, I hacked loose
the sluggy tongue, scooped
teaspoons of white, red–ribboned
brains free with fingernail,
knotted the carnage
into a postage stamp of plastic
to sear later, consider later.
What was mutilation,
what respect, what honoring
the appointed dead, I couldn't say.

HEART'S WARNING

Admit, these months
of ferocity scare you.
All year, desperate
within its cage of bone,
thundering at sheets,
ceaseless animal inside
vest. Every hour
you command it still,
will it to be calm,
and every attempt you fail.
Its announcement
an urgency of blood
you've repeated to no one,
not wife, not brother.
During the night's storm
was no different,
and now you listen again,
groggy and helpless
until your eyes burn
against a sky of ash
and another furious day
commencing. Easy,
old heart, don't panic.
The hands are hinges
of pain, but they may still
caress a lowered head
or hold a fist of salt.
The crooked back,
abused conspirator, may
lift a child to shoulders,
split wood for fire,

pour the black wine.
But your heart continues—
stark prophecy, wild
cadence, the gory future
that you hear it roar.

A Small, Gone Moment

Claudia kneels by the open doors
of the shed, filling long feeders
with a scoop, the center
around which the scene plays.

A tube of thistle for her goldfinches,
another oily sunflower
for cardinals, titmice, whatever arrives.
Both, of course, for the fat,

stub-tailed squirrel without respect.
Have I mentioned yet that Jasper
lopes round her in circles,
jerky, arthritic gestures

but happily in the action nonetheless?
Claudia wears her old green coat,
the thick cotton one I love
and sometimes slip into

though sleeves expose my wrists.
And yes, I'm there as well,
in the shadows of the porch
with a mug, waiting to be recognized

and waved to. It's a simple
moment among thousands,
lived only by the three of us,
only for us and the winter sun,

and I know with absolute certainty,
the instant tumbling through
my arms, that I'll never be happier,
never fuller, never again have

as much of what I want,
one small, gone moment
following another, until no more.
And all that sweet magic finished.

JASPER

Dear boy, it was you.
You with me in the house.
I don't know if I understood
it was dream or you were
dead. Beautiful, happy,

soft, white—the simple
inadequacies I return to.
I'm in France now,
stink-face, and Monday
you'll be gone from me

ten months. I gotta go,
too, the car is leaving
for the market. I'll buy meat
and bread and cheese—
good, hearty stuff you'd have

woofed, before you stopped.
I came from the dream
crying, like I am now,
a faint sky lightened
to the burden of another day.

Before I woke and left
you, you stood for me,
still brave within your pain.
You knew what I wanted—
to take up your body

to mine, to walk holding,
holding, holding tight,
until we reached the living
room, where your mother
waited just for us.

THE WALK

Sunday, la route de l'oignon

Two hours hard up the mountain,
we broke fast at shared tables—
eggs and raw onion, bacon, cheese,

bread. Always, wine for blood.
Bagpipers breathed sheeps' skins
into raucous, melancholy inflections.

Already it was time to move on,
singly, in pairs or clans, anxious
toward the stone tablet of the rooster,

L'etoile du Sambrès, over the top,
then down, down at various pace
to the village, to be conjoined again.

In the court of the old church
beneath flowered chestnuts,
we raised toasts to our good sense

in being here, to bodies held up
to the task, ate charred sausage.
The language that had brought us

few recalled—we mouthed the words
and cheered. Of course we danced,
sweaty circles holding fiercely

against the pull, one direction until
a human knot tightened, then back,
back loosening the other way.

The sun bore with us all the day,
just long enough, on fire in the bowls
of honey and our living faces.

SUNDAY, ANOTHER WEEK OF LIFE SPENT

> We lose everything, but make harvest
> of the consequence it was to us.
> —*Jack Gilbert*

My wash day. I pinned socks and shirts
and briefs between cropped chestnuts,
snapped photo with valley dropping behind.
What pleasure to not hear my voice
until evening. The house is Sunday quiet.

I sit or pace a room one thousand years old
and am neither happy nor unhappy,
lonely nor fully sufficient. A chainsaw
distracts from books—words can't contend.
I worry of indulgence at the grocer. Excess,

my métier. The confit, blood sausage,
duck breast, goat cheese, pasta and et cetera,
fresh small peas from the bent ancient
who gave me a generous reading of her
scales and weights. The mind's stinginess.

The saw stops. Already it is Sunday.
The *manoir* clings dusty and silent in centuries
navigated by swallows. Then cutting
inevitably resumes—the way things go.
I'll take an unknown path this afternoon,

any fine so long as it rises and tortures,
makes my bones moan and curse me.
I'll bathe, read, fold rags when they've dried.
This is how it's done, see, day to day,
something more or other than a blessing.

Later we'll gather at stove and table,
tooth the pink, briny shrimps brought over
the mountain yesterday from the sea,
fat stalks of local asparagus sautéed
in oil and garlic, eaten hot with the fingers.

And wine, the communal wine.
Then alone again I will think of my wife,
mother, father, entertain in darkness
any visiting shade as night closes over us
and blind stars still care for nothing.

Probably Human

Across the slow cage of hours
I paced, read, dozed, encouraged
clocks to move along, move along.
The martyrdom of stupid fabric,
my cottons, synthetics, delicates
on a drying line in the rain
perform the whole lovely futility.

On a desk, I arrange fragments
from yesterday's cold beach,
pearl contours, the dead polished
in grit and salt. Shards to foretell,
perhaps, some lie or truth we knew
or forgot. I finger each totem
and put it down.
                Preparation
for the afternoon's roughly turned
apologies, for night's practiced
and collateral damage—bare feet
bruised on stone, a cantata of glass,
as from the dark something heavy
falling, its single stifled shout.

After Twelve Songs for Morning, One for Night (or, Where Were You?)

The chapel darkened over my shoulder
as I let drop each empty bottle
to explode into the bin.
Bodies totaled thirteen, and I
attributed this to nothing special.
But it wasn't until I had wheeled
the cart back to the bastide,
bolted heavy door top and bottom,
and ascended the forty-eight steps
to my adequate room, not until, having
opened windows, discarded shoes,
unbuttoned shirt, and reclined
with both feet pointed
east toward the arriving night,
that the figure answered. As I sipped
an inch of earthy malt
and considered the sprawling contraction
of the world, a silhouette
took shape beside me on the bed.
And as I spoke aloud—indulgently, softly—
of where I had returned and what,
warily, I might still pray for to thunder,
the body assumed the full,
fleshy urgency of its darkness. Steady
cargo of cloud. Black spine of hill.
Brine and smoke on lips.
I held the golden liquid in my throat,
swallowed. I knew, if I had leaned
close then, breath hot in tangle
of hair invoked, across damp skin
summoned, if I had turned the vanishing
face to mine, it would be you.

LAST DAY

Simple rites and duties:
When the noon bells beckon,
lift your hat from its peg

and ascend once more
to the ridge of rock atop a world
you've already left behind.

Be grateful for patterns
of light, for wind that cools
and ships clouds south to the sea.

Appreciate durable legs
that brought you here
and arms that syncopate the way,

salt-sweat on lips. Don't speak.
Silence is refuge and virtue.
When you're ready,

when the hawk's dismissed you,
take the long valley pass,
path of beech and slate.

Above the village, serpentine,
come down then like God's own,
blessings for every family

of strangers at Sunday table.
The route back is a bear,
a bitch the whole way up,

but this after all is the last time,
and the toil, you know,
undoubtedly good for you.

Lost Poem Regarding the Musée d'Orsay, Rescued by Renoir

Somewhere in the dark enticements
of night that wondrous conceit arrived,
some mishap of the past contrasted
to a canvas in the special exhibit.
By morning, of course, this fine wisp
is lost, and not until I am walking in rain
do I recall to even try to remember
and strain toward two or three pairings
so facile, flimsy they're distasteful.
I'm pleased to be out early, returned
to the unexpectant grays of Cherbourg,
wind loosening knots of hot feeling,
unappeased downpour. A woman weighs
butter lettuce, radishes, three fistfuls
of *petit pois* in shell. At the *boulanger*,
where the girl, I believe, recognizes me,
I pretend to study her wooden racks
before choosing Monday's simple baguette.
Back in the flowing streets, my hands
pulse with cold, and as I consider
the arthritis beginning to stiffen knuckles,
glumly consider the future, I get lucky—
a rickety filmstrip begins of an old Renoir,
stick-thin Quixote in sloppy hat
and pointed white beard, the feral eyes,
brush wedged into a deformed root
once a human hand. Frames click past—
handle stabbed into stretched hole
of mouth, some startling atrocity of form
or light lunged at with a gnarled wrist,
brush clamped and parrying again.

What the Rain Taught

For days and weeks, finally months,
each sated hour pummeled color
from clothes, cold skin, left us silent,
heads bowed beneath dead sky,
vague regarding dreams we'd imported.

Finally, we left as we'd arrived,
fogged windows, lashing blades,
seats stuck to limp shoulders,
squinting toward melted landscapes.

Thinking back, those few
patches of blue, quickly smothered,
seemed a taunt of the life we'd planned
and thought deserved. Or, maybe,
just a memory of what we wasted
until the sun was gone.

FÊTE DE L'INDÉPENDANCE
(OR, JULY 4TH, FINAL EVENING IN FRANCE)

Forgive me, my compatriots,
if I reject the rusty hot dogs
and leather burgers of your grill,
forego smokes and sweaty beer.
Excuse me admiring further
your fresh flag and torpedo tattoos.

I'll be in my room upstairs,
you know where, slow-sautéing
in virgin oil a fat rabbit liver,
local onions properly caramelized,
half bottle of Languedoc red
all that's left before the early train.

Believe me, I celebrate with you
the tug and constraints of liberty—
it's strictly Bring Your Own
and no explosives allowed,
but just for fun, in a kindred spirit,
let's blow up something irreplaceable.

IV: THE DEAD METAPHORS

You're just a natural-born beehive
filled with honey to the top,
but I ain't greedy, baby,
all I want is all you got.
　　　—*Elvis Presley*

DEAD METAPHOR: CLOUDS

Reclined in a therapy of summer morning,
fishing the mackerel sky for answers,
is best avoided. No more wispy narratives

of cirrus, no cumulus caravan rolling fast
over static horizons. Trust this convective
of water vapor is not your dead father's mustache,

aerial mattress, or deconstructing dragon.
Merely traveling show of a billion crystals
equally reflecting all visible wavelengths of light,

aloft without premonition on currents of air
and unrelated to your "clouded" disposition
suddenly parted in serendipities of blue.

Accept the science as a blessing, as when,
one somber evening, a dark stratus of trouble
nearly touches ground, same grassy spot,

indeed, where you lay so dreamily, studying
a cottony Tarot of fair future. The roar
that's surely coming, foretold in ominous green

of cumulonimbus, sunlight fractured by ice,
whole doomed world suddenly twisting,
is not your problem, either. Take cover, relax.

DEAD METAPHOR: THE ROSE

How the room centers around a vase
centered on a table, narcotic loosening
of petals. My god, how quickly today passes,

beginning containing unfolded finish,
first beauty the solution to our pain,
whether wild thorn of woodside

or tended garden monarch—still dangerous
in her refinements—cut in the budding.
One petal, then another, silken flag,

proffered kerchief, dropped from soft knot,
lifted by hand and discarded upon
dappled stream of the mind, spun and parted.

Finis. For if that, faded lover, is the sort
of nonsense you incline to, please allow this
simple test: Lower your blushed face

into what remains of the flower's invitation,
press nose and lips to fragrant death. Inhale.
By any symbol, it smells as sweet.

DEAD METAPHOR: LEARNING THE BICYCLE

Cracked knees and elbows, bloodied chins,
don't make an archetype. There goes little Sally,
trainers off, she's—*uh-oh*—going down! *Ouch!*

Ho-hum. Tears and recriminations, question
of damaged trust. Next day typically comes next,
hard lessons again. Sally or Joey faring better,

wobble here, wobble there, maybe a tree leapt
in the way, but you will them up, will them safe,
and—*vóila!*—no casualties. Tedious victory

indulges tedious conceit, *to lead by following*,
or perhaps you merely gape into the circumstance
of empty arms. Joey's erect by himself now,

Sally's pumping for a whole street of watchful boys.
Or worse, it's young *you* on the banana seat,
clutching handlebars like a hell-raiser, risen high

and weaving straight (so to speak) into the future.
Dad's crouched back there somewhere,
but you've no time to turn, no need for advice.

Either story's the same: Once we master the trick
we never forget, then it's always kamikaze,
sayonara, always, *you tired old man, good-bye.*

DEAD METAPHOR: SUNLIGHT
AFTER MORNING THUNDER

The pristine azure, sudden ineluctable, edible
blaze. Darkened boughs against exhalation of green.
All the old materials sharpened by depth of field—

squirrel screeking, cardinal and jay, titter of goldfinch,
chickadee, baby wren. Water still dropping, predicate
and forceful, into stippled shade. *Yadda yadda,*

you say, *a lost cause,* to the wild rose fully offered,
honeysuckle, common privet, umbrella of clematis
opened late. You've stalked and talked this landscape

to death, until you're either red in the face or blue,
yet beckoned over drowsing dog, through storm door,
out of slippers and into it, the spongy, muddy mess,

stalks shining between toes, solar fire on face,
neck and arms, arching to that trite rock,
feels too damned good to make it anything at all

except what it marvelously is, too late to salvage
syntax or fail again to name it, whatever the hell *it* is.
Be grateful, baboon. Big dumb mammal. Breathe.

Dead Metaphor: Home

Forth and back with the mower, back, forth,
fevered trail of tears across July, August, into fall,
direction without arrival, rows as sculpted

as a cemetery's every third day, with lots of time
to think, if you'd something to think about.
In the kitchen, up to elbows in vaporous gray

sludge, ocean of plate, glass, flatware/flotsam
washed to a greasy shore of counter
day by day, hour by hour, with opportunity again

to reflect: out a porthole of window
(badly requires paint), through torn screen
(begs for scrub and hose), across the green sea,

alien, unconquerable, neat waves faded already,
tempestuous fins rising hungrily
for sun. Obliquely, if one strains and cares to,

one may note deck railing (screams for stain),
anchor of mortgage crashed through
a mildewed hull. A door slams and your Love

lowers the lifeboat for a splash into the world.
The raft's on 60 months, zero down, same as cash.
A ship's a dead metaphor, too. But it still sinks.

Dead Metaphor: Pregnant Wife

Pardon graceless title. We know to you
her girth was luminous, even most contrary
moods and demands to your ear playful.

How you couldn't stop fondling the moon
of her stomach, measuring mule bucking
inside, holding seismographic ear against taut skin.

Couldn't stop staring over the frame of your book
even when she asked you, seriously, to stop.
We know you sat on the floor cradling feet,

thought of Jezebel and the Bible, forgave yourself
jumbled similes, ideas in fact a joyful mess.
This no time to think straight, you thought,

proved it repeatedly through nine months.
Yes, we know the beauty that has overtaken
can't be adequately spoken, sacrifice makes it better,

nothing's shameful in goofiness or prayer.
God would keep her safe, you were certain
He/She would, and that writhing, bellowing,

red-faced monstrosity—so beyond language—
you raise tearfully, humbly to hospital scrubs,
that's your legacy, *raison d'être*, the whole

loaded enchilada of life's exquisite purpose,
sapling to your roots. Something like that.
Daddy, daddy, no more tom-foolishness for you.

Here's the digitally edited, high-def DVD—
fully scored to your lover's contractions—
documenting the whole bloody miracle, all for us.

DEAD METAPHOR: ILLNESS

Amalgam of day, attenuated night.
Slab of blanket and sheet you strain
beneath, limbs curled in hopeless defense.

Teeth literally chattering in your head,
head angled on pillow of stain.
This, dream deserved, dream earned,

bad end—house where you were raised
filled with suspecting, unkind faces,
key useless in lock, the great tree felled.

Your kid brother, gone twenty years,
turns from a plea of forgiveness.
Teeth rattle the bone language,

rough dice in a bowl of skull. *One chance,*
one more, you squeak, trite Scrooge
negotiating his surrogate darkness.

The world will see a man reborn it won't
believe. You believe, though, long enough
at least to implore ambiguous angels

who teach their lessons the old way,
to mumble through cracked, penitent lips,
Deliver me, and I will sin no more.

DEAD METAPHOR: FIDELITY

Anyway, you know you've too much
to lose, plus it's convenient to trust
and be trusted, right? Nothing as practical

as idealism: Sleeping only by him or her—
gaseous pardons, endearing rhonchus—
you sleep most soundly with yourself.

So what if heyday in the blood is tamed,
so what if you're humbled. You know
there's judgment, too, to wait upon.

And what judgment allows step from this
to that? Two old boots sagged in the closet.
Infrequent hand in a loose glove.

Still, isn't it nice just to be together?
No deceit and all that backhand history?
You know any charm outside four walls

is siren song, first-order Circe or Charybdis.
Soft lie of lips, arm grazing hip and so on,
exist anymore as grainiest abstraction,

small-screen banality. The dark hot
release? The dizzying, drowning center?
Come on. You know better than that.

Dead Metaphor: Infidelity

Your boys accosting soccer field, fierce
and whole, would never forgive the selfishness,
fathom need. Good God, how to explain?

Now it's load'm up, back to the Volvo,
back in the grid of eternal chauffeuring,
vision blurry behind prescription shades.

Next game, next camp, next drive-through.
This bourgeois façade of your true life,
private and panicked. For you, of all people,

have taken a lover. "Lover"! Christ,
you're in Chekhov! Those business "retreats"
to Yalta. Ah, interminable Moscow,

routine and dreary. You're a stunned
secret sharer, heart frantic at narrow timetables,
ringing telephones, lost slip of paper.

Head abuzz with physics of deniability.
Even your name hangs tight in the shoulders,
loose at the hips, and your face, reflected

in a dull, sweet, undeserving spouse's—
does he suspect?—over another strained meal,
is a dark stranger. You could never, ever

have an affair, you explained that afternoon
in the hotel. Never live a lie or convince with it,
you clarified a second time, quieter,

as the other pursued your unbuttoning.
This was madness! Dream and nightmare!
I cannot tell a lie, you mumbled again,

as the cherry tree went promptly down
and you stroked the Delaware together
toward some terrible, rapturous new country.

Dead Metaphor: Bullfighting

Literature that read realer than the real thing:
hot Spanish afternoons, cool *fino* at a café table
as hucksters and dark gypsies congregated,

tapas of pickled squid, manchego, *jamón*,
tripe in olive oil. Young men are suckers
for myth and ritual, gory details, hard seat

above the *callejón* watching handlers for truth.
Now you'd be hard-pressed between *pase de pecho*
and limp *veronica*, Manolete versus El Cordobés.

But some language lingers, as from dead sleep
this morning you opened near-sighted eyes
toward the dog panting in his narrow *querencia*

beside fern and bay window. Approach at risk!
Or when, hip thrust under one fist, the other
guiding your new blood-red leaf blower

as if *muleta* over killing sword, you realize, *torero*,
this as good as it's likely to get. What relief
vocabulary fades to the preposterous. Courage?

Not wheeling the overheated Toyota off a bridge.
Ritual? Hand tight on the goddamn remote.
Myth? That young man used to think, without

a *copita* of irony, maybe *toro bravo* was the story:
Five years of wild freedom, savage king
of an unspoiled hill country. Fifteen minutes

of *sol y sombra* doing what you were built for.
Then definitive death. Bull, alright. *Olé!*
Leaves leap in terror. The dog goes back to sleep.

DEAD METAPHOR: DAY LILIES

The crisp snap of each neck as you collect yesterday's
prizes in two hands—monument of dripping mush.
Today's today, another morning of inventory and praise,

frank confession regarding favorites, who's having
banner year, who disappoints. The sexy language
lily geeks adore: stigma, style, pollen-heavy anthers.

Ritual hook of loss and renewal. Avant Garde's
last day, a single preening bloom. By afternoon,
June sun will pale her lemon throat to ivory,

then brief and angry storm shred apricot petals.
It's a tough life, ya know, gone in a blink. Impossible
to hold perfection, rare a long good-bye. Today's today:

first of Bengaleer, her lanky, lion-gold curves.
Labial midribs of Ballerina embarrass you to look,
but you do. Call Girl just spreading peach enticements—

she doesn't like to open early. How can you resist
the action, aroused caretaker in shorts and slippers?
Shades of color—carmine, scarlet, strawberry rose . . .—

shades of temperament—tall scape or short, head demure
or brash into sky—enliven your private converse.
Jutting hello of Lusty Leland, White Tie Event's

exquisite ruffle. Scotsboro's pink beyond delicacy.
When I Dream, my god you're a fiery wench, but
Fair Annette's back tomorrow, and you know how I feel

about her blowsy, butter-cream languor. She's obvious I know,
but I can't help myself. By now, Little Ginger's bleeding
down your arms and you've stained another t-shirt

with fistfuls of dead-head goo you're still squeezing.
You spiral the mess over compost, Thursday's 72 affairs
atop the day before's, forgotten. Friday to follow.

DEAD METAPHOR: MOSQUITOES AS NAZIS

Spanish diminutive of *mosca*, or fly,
Latin *musca*, but you're thinking only *mein Gott!*
as a phalanx of needle-nosed *Luftwaffe*,

gray-striped, fat black, maneuver and close in.
Battalion of thirsty sorrows. You complete
a Chaplinesque retreat across cracked earth,

reeling from friendly fire of hard slaps,
neck, ankles aflame already in terrain of welts.
On your hands, ashen stains of casualties,

smears of blood. Nice. High summer,
the battle rages, living's fierce. You swig
from a tepid bottle, contemplate the grill,

slam yourself in the throat. Too slow, *mein freund*.
Then the bottle again, buzz in the ears.
Dazing coruscations of heat. West Nile

running your veins. You exposed yourself
to admire the grass-cutting theatre of operations,
tactical successes. But to hell with the front.

You can lament your homeland under siege
from air-conditioned bunker, inside out.
Surrender the field. Gas the chicken.

DEAD METAPHOR: THE NUMBER THIRTEEN

Triskaidekaphobe, triskaidekaphile, let's call
the whole thing off. But you can't, can you?
Thirteenth day of every worrisome month,

thirteen rungs of the ladder you've no choice
but slip beneath. Black cat high-assing
thirteen steps across the fateful highway

you've just entered. Scratch your neck
thirteen times and feel the wooly noose.
Call it baker's dozen of gloom and get on with it.

A relief, really, this controlling chance at work
explanation for all your considerable luck,
all bad. Perhaps with a lifetime's practice,

ten incantations plus tongues of toad (three),
or the right number (any notion?) of runes
asymmetrical inside thirteen ecstatic candles,

you can forward the fun to your best enemy.
But no, here he is now at the head of table,
clinking crystal as you're ushered in for the finale:

Twelve seated and you're number guess what?
Happy 39th birthday (13 + 13 + etc. . . .) to you.
Chorus well-deserved, guy. Last Supper indeed.

DEAD METAPHOR: POST-DIVORCE HARLEY-DAVIDSON

Road King, Electra Glide, mystic invocation.
Sure, she and the mouthpiece stole house
and Hyundai, got manicured claws into 401K,

plucked you, frankly, like a limp duck.
What did you get? F-R-E-E-D-O-M, brother,
and why not buy a vowel and just name it

"Free Doom." Fate of the wild road, forgotten
America, Route 40 all the way to Barstow,
that thunder between your legs the right massage

to grow balls back before you tour through
accessorized in leather and chrome to claim
your lordly position in the City of Angels,

ample room for company on stitched seat.
She clipped your wings for too, too many years,
but the devil's hard disciple will fly again.

Or maybe Vegas would be good, even Flagstaff.
Hell, any place but here, this musty apartment
in Shit Town. You're undercover, in the cave,

practicing once more for the magic mirror
your jacket and skully, biker wallet with chain.
Sure, they delivered the Harley, your test run

cracked fence and left you bruised and shaking.
Fear, power; power, fear. Why even unpack?
You'll be history long before six-month lease.

Tomorrow, then, to rumble parking lot.
Sure, so what if those punks you pass all think
the same: *Hey, look at that old guy on that hog.*

Dead Metaphor: The Champagne Toast

To *auld lang syne* and good riddance, to thirty
slaughtered years for steady profit of the Company.
To the bride. To 400 million bubbles per bottle,

effervescent river of dreams. To lowered daggers,
hearty wishes, five centuries of evil spirit warned
with a clink of cup. To getting toasted, more next year,

better next time, chartable progress in long Cha Cha
off a short pier. To Frère Jean and Dom Pierre,
orders of Pierry and Epernay. To the 17th century.

To 1836, *Method François*, mountains of milestones
to pass. To Veuve Cliquot, Tattinger, a Spanish cheapie,
it's all good. To your happy, sponging tongue.

To a quick buzz and quick squeeze, not safe nor sorry,
your consummate recovery and comeback.
Palms itchy? You're falling into some coin, fella.

Feet as well? Somebody's two-stepping across a grave.
Well you can't have it all, all the time. (*Can* you?)
"May ye live as long as ye want to, and want to

long as ye live," waxed your Irish uncle, ubiquitous
glass in hand. Then he walked over all the graves,
all the way to Alaska, never came back. Cheers.

V: Otra Vez

In Spain, the dead are more
alive than the dead in any
other country in the world.
—*Federico García Lorca*

HYMN OF THE FLIES

Orchestrated in the ears,
treacly sheen of the face,
prairie of the arms.

They arrive where
you arrive, on either side
of a worthless screen

or frantic on the bitten trail,
another god to devour.
They come singing.

Slap yourself, and again,
a welting percussion.
One crushed life

returns as two, as four,
as twelve. The body stumbles—
their hungry attentions

keep it moving.
At the ears again
the frantic hard music,

mission song against skin.
Choir of flesh, chorus of blood.
What choice but accept

this brutal worship,
cross with muttered curses—
a hopeless prayer to the wind.

For Now, Rise

Perhaps you still control it,
perhaps already the choice is ceded.
What difference? Either way,
night is still night. No bird mimics,

no wind relieves this desert where
you've arrived. You're through
with astrologies and gypsy nonsense.
Bring on a bitter end. You'll conjure

your despair once too often
and stay there, just dumb enough
to wonder when the ceiling fell,
when the door slammed shut for good.

Not yet. Hell, perhaps you can live
like this forever. When sky
lightens and the blade of moon is lost,
that still means it's morning.

Better yet the Sabbath, best day
for rising from self-destruction.
Start rising. Clothe thyself
in the robes and scarves of loathing

required by your cockeyed church.
Dry damp touch of dream
from forehead. A commandment
hammers there. Listen. Rise up.

Strap on cracked sandals. Your shame's
out where you left it. Wanderer,
seek it out. Pretend, for now,
this could happen any other way.

THE FREAK OF GRANADA

Black-footed and bone-chested,
red shorts slipping down a scrawny ass,
and sunglasses, stolen or cajoled,
wrapping bald head. Most of us,
tourists, had sweated stone steps
to the height of the Moorish quarter—
Alhambra looming into evening,
mountains behind, sparkling city below.
To watch the guitarist
and each other. With your bulbous
clown's eyes and thin, elastic face,
you spied a group of young Brits
and closed in, appointed yourself friend
and trickster. The poor, pretty girl
at the end, unrescued by the boy
beside her, took the brunt of rambling
and practiced goofiness.
She was too young, too kind,
too frightened to send you to hell.
Not panhandling exactly, just borrowed
cigarette, shared bottle of beer. Business
about a magnifying glass retrieved
from your backpack, uproarious effect
of peering through into sky.
More eye-rolling and rubber-facing.
The kids didn't know what it or you meant
but bought in with another swig.
You couldn't sit still, worked the plaza,
jittery routine on every vendor
save a monolithic brick of old woman

expressionless with canastas.
Even a fool knows his match.
I thought: How simple to shoulder you
over retaining wall into broken angles
in the alley below. No identity,
an unclaimed mess. I hated you,
my hostility at what I saw I recognized.
How quick, complete that fall would be.

OCCASIONAL

47 years ago this morning Hemingway
shot himself. The year was '61, he was 61,
a meaningless coincidence.

Today I returned to Spain. I drank whisky,
feet bare on warm evening stones
of a courtyard nonexistent 13 years ago.

Numbers: On 3 April this year I was 43.
If the pattern holds, and it won't,
I will return here at 56, at 69, then . . . well.

Today is no one's birthday I know
that I am aware of. Rest assured many
are making the best or worst of it.

I have lived longer than Jesus, Elvis,
even Chekhov, although some would
argue the point regarding Jesus.

My oldest brother would, a minister
in Cincinnati. His birthday next week.
I've not seen him in years, know no address.

Four days later, 14 July, Jasper
will be dead two years.
I have dreamed of him three nights running.

This my first poem in precisely six months.
I was in India then, tallying numbers,
pledging to ghosts our nascent year of 2008.

Winter and spring were disgraceful.
So I am in Spain, given another chance,
as Hemingway was in 1959. Failed, apparently.

Two Years

You will never again tremble
through that bloody morning.
For this I am grateful.
How you suffered to stay with us.
A storm began today at 5:20 a.m.
I listened dumbly for hours,

no reply to offer. Water shocked
brittle earth, polished gray
leaves bright. But not enough
to save anything needing saving.
When I crossed the valley at noon,
cautious neighbor dog decided

I was friend and trotted along.
I'm keeping from human company
today. You're the one I'd
confide in, whose joy I crave
a taste of. And to the pitiless sky
I confess again I couldn't

take your pain away, or heal.
I'm sorry I kept you living
unbearably. But baby, baby,
I couldn't let go until no choice.
I wanted every selfish minute.
Yesterday I called your mother

to remind her to buy flowers—
cut, potted, whatever nicest—
to spend quiet time on the bench

between the blue hydrangeas,
reciting to you again, then again,
all the old, obvious things.

BUCKET LIST

No parachutes, Mt. McKinley,
heights of any kind.
No gator wrestling, shark baiting,
tent with grizzlies. No Maserati.
Nothing so easily achieved.

Sure, more gardening in spring
as first small fists green and open,
more books, moons, dark wine,
to get to love another good dog.
The soul of the list, though,

contains all that can't be done
or undone, roads mistaken,
others I wasn't ready for.
To get the act of my life together
sooner, more completely,

keep everything longer
than I had it. A crazy, savage
greed. There I am at sunset
at our ample cabin in France,
clown in beret delivering

pitcher and glasses to terrace.
There my parents, healthy
and laughing, perhaps even fluent
grandson between them.
Those views, that delicious light!

Never thought they'd see *this*, eh?
All the hours in the world
for our dinner, Claudia unleashing
course after murderous course
as Jasper stays close to help.

And I to the side signing
in blood my poorly bartered
pact to hold the day. *More time,*
more, more. Unfortunately
for me, the devil doesn't exist.

SMALL MERCY

Claudia, here the slow heat smothers
afternoon. I close windows and doors,
in shadow appreciate how consummately
I have defeated the day and myself.
I think of your day beginning,
your early movement through the rooms
of the house. I would be grateful
to speak with you. Not to fail again to explain
everything I understand less and less,
but to learn the names of the blooming
lilies, safety of baby rabbit and turkey,
construct your mood by tone of voice.
To amuse, I might mention the scorpion
trapped and let loose this morning,
but not my trembling left hand, the fear
I recite like a prayer, how the night was.
In the plaza, I fell as others rose in applause.
Strangers placed me onto unsteady feet.
I never again want to see such faces of concern.
You've heard these apologies before,
patiently, hopeful so many years.
I won't call. A small mercy I can grant.
But if I could, I would like to explain
so we both understood why I swore twice
to you I would not return to this place,
then returned, what I listen for in my breath,
what fevered lesson dreams conceal.
I wrote, "I have destroyed my life to live it."
That young man is gone. I've no theory on
his passing. I witness nothing, recall nothing,
confident only of this steady diminishing.

I intended to return to you complete,
healed, a husband you could joyfully claim.
Truly I did. In what's left of the hours here
my throat tightens, my lungs flame.
Claudia, if I could only convince us
it was me, I would call whether or not
I deserved the privilege of your attention.
Is there any chance on earth that, after all,
all will be well? I am dying to believe so.

SCALLOPING

Did we enjoy that day? You indulged me.
Hundreds of fiddlers scuttled collectively
as I forced the kayak into the bay,
steadied it for you to take first seat.

Lord, that August was hostile, ferocious,
even the spray hot as I paddled us out
among strange flora, past horseshoe crab,
primordial, armored, a wide dark plate.

Into thicker water. I dropped our diving
flag and flopped starboard. Snorkel and fins,
alien dream undulating inches away.
You didn't want it, sat bobbing at anchor,

reading, burning. Below the surface,
your hesitance and worry—rowed too far,
landscape indistinguishable, how would we
navigate against tide?—disturbed

the creature a husband had morphed to,
its aqueous world. No legal license,
the creature brought up clawfuls of clamping
shells as offering, forced stiff hinges,

ate briny bodies for your amusement.
You weren't amused. I descended for more,
a few, but the fun was over. Nothing
quite works, hope sinks, we both knew that.

Still—our rented cabin awaited, private
strip of peninsula. Cool bath and drinks,
the pier's gangly congregation of pelicans
that reliably pleased. The more or less

promise of evening. Salty with sweat,
sea, smallness, face and neck crepuscular red,
I muscled us to shore by the clear division
between cypress, no problem at all.

SIESTA FOR THE DYING

Perhaps a few disconnected flashes—
snow turning in wet flakes
over that first winter in the house,
a sweet spoon of dessert
or a French market flooded with light,
weighing radish and cherry.

Mostly though, as I lie in a room
as dim as this, prostrate on similarly
creased and sweated sheets,
I'll recall my mother and father,
try to conjure their lost faces,
smile at my grinning dog in the ground

for decades. My wife, hollow
from crying, will hold my hand
lightly so not to hurt. I'll offer banalities
of comfort that bring none,
whisper for water, tally a typical math
of regret and disbelief—*how can this be?*

And yes, as open eyes go blind
and last breath exhales a ghost,
as the exhausted heart surrenders,
yes I will think of you, remember you,
and that for me will be the end.

ERNESTO'S 109TH BIRTHDAY PARTY

I wrote in the morning, not badly,
then walked the long walk
to beach and floated for amusement,
swam hard against the current
and back with it. Sand burned.

The old man's in my head again,
perhaps because I am surprised
to return to Spain, indulging errors
I thought I'd corrected,
perhaps black and white photos—
defeated body, sad fortune-teller's eyes—
of the last completed summer.

Festivities unraveled into night,
as festivities should. Beaded sangria,
roasted chicken al fresco
from two greasy fists, crisp skin
and moist flesh. Sunset
behind the mountain where the old town
fell to pieces. Earth claimed the ruin.

No one came, not even a wraith.
Light failed, the mountain
darkened into threat
beneath a hung moon. Last toast
to end the last party,
and the wavering lights of Garrucha
candles marking a broken coast.

FOR BEATRIZ, BELÉN, AND BEATRIZ MARÍA

As they assault the courtyard
studio by studio—quick knocks,
warning *holas*, clanking buckets
and mops—a small poem
about last night's scorpion dream
withers and dies. Cleaning Day.
I shred the page and wait.
When my time comes, I return
a quick greeting and get out.
I've considered before
these sturdy, elusive women
who cook for me, wash and hang
undergarments on demand,
attend general needs of comfort
so I may sit in a pillowed chair
and imagine my songs of longing.
Songs in a language to them
gibberish. When Belén,
or Beatriz María, possibly Beatriz
exits with a rustle of trash—
torn revisions, cookie wrappers,
toiletry unmentionables—and latches
the screen, I am back in business.
I follow to the kitchen for
a wave and superfluous *gracias*,
then, excited, cross the threshold
into shady, bleach-clean privacy.
I touch the pristine altar of bed,
press my face to a towel.
The basket yawns for more waste.
Wet tiles, meanwhile, await

footprints from daily nuptials
with the goddess of beach
and muse of the sea. Thank you
ladies. You'll never read this
and not miss much, but I go now
to pursue my end of a bargain.
Of course, I'll be starved for dinner
and the red wine you'll chill.

A History of Flamingos

Comically, impossibly thin
and misjointed legs, hooked beak,
flash of hot pink under wing.

Not two million en masse
screeching Lake Nakuru. Even so.
I sit alone in the blind,

glassing across salt flats
in mid morning, relying
on my good eye. Brine dazzles,

diamond coruscations
blurring the thousand weird,
migrating shapes. No one's

in a hurry. How freeing to leave
others stranded, feel no guilt,
even a possibility of beginnings,

that life needn't only narrow
to inevitable losses.
Or so flamingos murmur.

If I looked away from birds
reposed on single stilts,
contracting to feathered ovals

as heat arrives, probably
I could see at curb a tiny car,
hired one day only for whatever

can be claimed. Straight miles
of blank sand preceding body count.
Beyond that: *azul profundo.*

How fine my dawn escape,
wheels spitting gravel, country
yawning, owl on a wire.

Adventure without interference,
with horoscope support—
"Let anyone tell you differently!"

Further, austere beauty
of Cabo de Gata, volcanic ridge,
secluded bays for the daring.

Not Costa Rica *wow*, but still.
A key in a shirt pocket
and first trace sweat of the day.

READING TED HUGHES ON THE BEACH, LAST DAY IN SPAIN

1. *The dark ate at you. And the fear / Of being crushed.*

Sky a blue sail all the way around
the cove. When I sit up, arms and calves
stuccoed with sand, I squint south
and see, distinct miles away,
the white houses of the pueblo.

2. *A fistula of smouldering bitumen. / Hellish.*

Volcanic mountains edge the beach,
prickly but benign. Sunday afternoon.
I watch a yellow flag flirting
toward sea just calm enough for play,
rough enough for mischief.

3. *Your undertow withdrawal / Blinded and choked you.*

Drowsy with lunch and wine, I rise,
stumble into surf, hold my own
then dive for cool, clear brilliance,
swim out, spin and float,
toes curled in Mediterranean air.

4. *Our lives were still a raid on our own good luck.*

Reclined again and dripping,
I look up from the damp text
to admire four women, darkly tanned,
in black bikinis, teething the fullest,
most dazzling peaches I have ever seen.

THE BLACK RUBY

Shut the door to laughter,
guard shadow and silence.
Resist all solicitation,
every brutal kindness.

Let tribe perfect self-tribute,
chatter and drone. Smile.
Commit to nothing
save your timed withdrawal.

Look to the sky, study
scarred bowl of hands
for answer. Decline again
each offer of citizenship.

Behind secure walls,
you will find their venom
sweet, anger a cooling balm.
Stay. I will feed you

as I have fed upon you.
We shall continue, faceted
always in our dark light,
one glorious crystal blood.

BIOGRAPHICAL NOTE

GAYLORD BREWER's most recent books are his 8th poetry collection, *Give Over, Graymalkin* (Red Hen Press, 2011), and the comic novella *Octavius the 1st* (Red Hen Press, 2008). Earlier books of poetry include *Presently a Beast* (Coreopsis Books, 1996), *Devilfish* (Red Hen Press, 1999; winner of the inaugural Benjamin Saltman Poetry Prize), *Four Nails* (Snail's Pace Press, 2001; winner of the 2001 Snail's Pace Poetry Prize), *Barbaric Mercies* (Red Hen Press, 2003), *Exit Pursued by a Bear* (Cherry Grove Collections, 2004), *Let Me Explain* (Iris Press, 2006), and *The Martini Diet* (Dream Horse Press, 2008; winner of the 2006 Orphic Prize). His critical works include *David Mamet and Film* (McFarland, 1993) and *Charles Bukowski* (Macmillan, 1997). He has published 800 poems in journals and anthologies, such as *Best American Poetry* and *The Bedford Introduction to Literature*, and his plays have been staged in Chicago, Columbus, Nashville, New York, and Valdez, Alaska. Among his recent residencies were the Global Arts Village (India) and Can Serrat and the Fundación Valparaíso (both in Spain). Brewer, a native of Louisville, Kentucky, earned a Ph.D. from Ohio State University. He is a professor at Middle Tennessee State University, where he founded and edits the journal *Poems & Plays,* and has also taught in Russia, Kenya, and the Czech Republic. In 2009, he was awarded an Individual Artist Fellowship in Poetry from the Tennessee Arts Commission.